OVERCOMER

*Discovering God's Plan
Against All Odds*

DORSEY ROSS

ISBN: 978-0-578-72578-9 (paperback)

Contents

INTRODUCTION

Dad was born on May 12, 1931 in Bangor, Maine. He was raised in a family with five brothers and five sisters, not including himself. Four years later, on May 3, 1935, Mom was born to Anna and Dorsey Short, who I would later be named after. Mom had a brother and a sister. Her brother was also named Dorsey, so my name really runs in the family. Who knows? Maybe if I ever have kids, I will name my son Dorsey, just to have the name continue in the family.

Dad was a Marine and was on emergency leave to visit his nephew, Billy. He was walking through Jamaica, NY when he came across Mom. He saw her walking with one of her girlfriends down Jamaica Avenue. He asked her if he could have some of her ice cream, and she said, "No, get your own!" They continued talking, and eventually, she did decide to give him some of her ice cream. Three months later, on December 7, 1952, they got married. They never had a honeymoon, though. That's because Dad got deployed and went off to fight in the Korean War.

We all experience surprises at some point, whether it's a birthday party we didn't know about, a gift we didn't expect to get, a surprise proposal, or a trip someone takes us on.

Have you ever had the shock of that pregnancy test coming out positive, even though you weren't expecting to have another baby? Imagine that you already had two grown daughters and that you had gone through two other pregnancies, but these babies had died a few weeks after birth. My parents had already experienced this situation. The two babies they had lost would have been my older brothers. Then, a couple of decades later, they found out there was a surprise heading their way in several months.

My mom started to gain weight, and she decided to go to the doctor. Because of her age, she thought that she could possibly have a tumor growing inside of her. You see, my parents were up in age. Dad was forty-five, and Mom was forty-one, so they were definitely not expecting to have another baby. When the doctors tested my mom, the results came back conclusive that she was pregnant. For all that I have been through in my life, I'm thankful that I wasn't a tumor, but a baby boy growing inside of my mom.

Several months later, on a cold, snowy January morning, Mom went into labor and had to be taken to Jamaica Hospital in Queens, New York. On Sunday, January 16, 1977, several hours after her arrival at the hospital, she gave birth to the baby she had waited months to finally see.

Think back to the time when you had your first child, or imagine you just gave birth to a son or daughter. What was the first thing you did or wanted to do? Like most people, you wanted to hold your baby, even if it was for a few seconds. You wanted to see the baby's eyes, and you wanted to make sure without a doubt that the baby was healthy, even if he or she was crying. You just wanted to see your baby.

Unfortunately, that didn't happen for my parents. They weren't able to see me. The doctors had to rush me off to be examined. What they saw was a baby whose forehead was pushed outward, whose eyes and nose were pushed inward, and whose fingers and toes were fused, meaning I had no individual movement of them.

It was later discovered that I had Apert Syndrome, which is a rare congenital defect that only happens in one in 65,000 to 200,000 births. I've often wondered if the doctors had known or even seen a baby with my type of birth defect before.

The doctors were very matter-of-fact with my parents. They said, "We can't take care of him. There is nothing we can do. We know this isn't something you wanted to hear, but unfortunately, your newborn baby will not survive."

One of the most severe problems with Apert is that babies have no soft spot or skull opening on their head, which would stop their brain from growing. Since I did not have a soft spot, the doctors informed my parents that I would eventually become brain dead. They said the best option for them would be to sign the papers and put me into an institution.

Let's stop right there for a second. Imagine going

through nine months of pregnancy, hours of labor, and finally giving birth to a baby. Then, a few days later, the doctors hand you papers to sign, encouraging you to give up on him. Their reason? Because they're quite sure the baby isn't going to make it. For parents, this is probably a worst-case scenario, never mind *my* parents, who had already lost two sons at birth because of different disabilities. My parents were probably thinking, *Not again! We can't go through this again! What is happening here?*

They were very confused about what they should do. For years, my parents had been going to a church in Richmond Hill, Queens, called Bethlehem Assembly of God. A few days after I was born, they went and spoke to their pastor, William Behr, to get some guidance. He replied that he couldn't tell them what to do, but that he would pray for them. He didn't say, "Well, you should bring him home. It will be an easy road. Don't worry about it." Instead, he told them to pray and seek God, and then to do what God told them.

After I was born, my dad walked down a hallway by himself to ask God what he should do. Should he give up on a child that God had just given him? He didn't know what to do, but God did.

The Holy Spirit spoke to Dad and said, "Be still."

The first time I heard that story, I thought of Psalm 46:10, which says, "Be still and know that I am God" (NIV). I am not sure what my father would have done if God hadn't spoken to him in that dark hallway, but I am sure glad that He did.

Although the most severe symptoms are of the face and hands, Apert also affects other parts of the body, whether at birth or later in life. Apert often causes slower learning rates and sweating a lot during the night. I did not learn as fast as my classmates when I was in school.

I have read other articles on Apert Syndrome that have listed more severe symptoms, such as fusion of the vertebrae in the neck, crossed eyes, underbite, extra fingers and toes, noisy breathing and developmental delays. Even though I experienced some symptoms, I have felt fortunate because I could've been much worse.

A lot of people may have been angry with God or may have even cursed God that they had been born this way, especially with this severity of Apert Syndrome. However, somehow, I was able to recognize that God allowed me to be born the way I was for a reason and a purpose. It definitely wasn't easy to come to that conclusion, and I didn't come out of the womb thinking that way. It took me quite a long time to realize that regardless of what I was going to go through in this life, God allowed me to have Apert Syndrome because He had something in store for me – more than I could have ever dreamed or imagined.

You will hear me say that a lot throughout this book. I say it because that is what I truly believe. God didn't say, "I am going to make Dorsey a person with a disability to punish him or to hurt him and his parents." My parents did nothing wrong. God allowed this to happen because He knew He had a plan and a purpose for my life and my parents' lives. I have heard a lot of people say that their circumstances are all God's fault. They blame God for things that have happened to them when it's really no one's fault; things just happen sometimes in life. Thankfully, my parents didn't blame God. They didn't argue with Him and ask, "Why us? Why would you allow this to happen to us?"

I know one thing – if I were in my father's shoes, I would have been scared out of my mind. Maybe someday I will face the same thing he did, because if I were to get married, there is a 50/50 chance of passing on this disability to my children. I honestly don't know if I would want to take the chance of passing on Apert, but that is a decision my wife and I will have to make if God chooses for me to get married. I have seen what I have gone through in my life, and I don't know if I would want to see my son or daughter go through that. Regardless of what happens, and if I do have a child with Apert, I will love that child, just as my parents loved me.

1

OVERCOMER

In the end, my parents never signed the papers.

I am fortunate to have parents who believed in a God who is bigger than the human beings who told them their son wouldn't survive.

Too many times, we hear what our doctors say and take it as law. The doctors might say that your cancer has spread and there's nothing they can do. They might say that your tumor has gotten bigger. Because this is what the doctor says, we think all is lost, we are hopeless, and we will never be healed. However, we must remember that God says in Exodus 15:26, "For I am the LORD, your Healer." I want to encourage you today – God is still a miracle-working God. We need to believe by faith that miracles still happen today, and they have happened in my own life. A lot of people say that I am a walking miracle because of all that I have been through. I have definitely seen God's miracles take place in my life.

For example, one time I was dealing with a numbing

sensation on my right side. This sensation would only last for a few seconds at a time before going away. I went to the doctor and found out I had a pinched nerve and fused vertebrae in my neck. The doctor told me that because the issue wasn't severe, we wouldn't do anything. I'm glad he decided to go this route. Since the injury was on my neck and near my spine, I did not want him to touch it unless there was an emergency. I prayed about the issue, and after a while, it went away. I believe by faith that God miraculously healed me.

One of my favorite Bible stories is about Paul's thorn in the flesh, because I can relate to it. Three different times, Paul cries out to God to remove this annoying thorn that he has in his side. We do not know exactly what Paul's thorn was. It may have been metaphorical, but mine is mostly physical. The definition of a thorn is something that wounds, annoys, or causes discomfort. This is definitely something I don't want in my life!

However, at some point, we all have to deal with "thorns." We've all gone through some difficulties, if we're honest. We deal with different types of thorns, including spiritual, physical, mental, and emotional. When you've had these experiences, maybe you've questioned God. Why now? What did I do to deserve this?

Some of the biggest thorns I have faced in my life have been the insults of others, all the operations I've endured, and frequent visits to the doctor. I don't love getting stuck with needles or having IVs in my arm. Being content means taking pleasure in something, and I don't take pleasure in these things. I don't think I will ever be excited about going to the doctor or needing a blood test.

Nevertheless, I am encouraged by 2 Corinthians 12:9: "And [God] has said to me, 'My grace is sufficient for you, for power is perfected in weakness.' Most gladly, therefore, I will rather boast about my weaknesses, so that the power of Christ may dwell in me" (NASB). When we are weak, when we don't have the strength to keep moving forward, or when we feel like giving up on life, God is the One who will give us the strength to go on. Have there been times when you have felt like giving up because of the thorn in your flesh?

Regardless of what your thorn might be, I want to encourage you today not to give up, not to submit to the weaknesses that you may be suffering. Instead, cry out to God and ask Him to give you the strength to keep on going. Consider this for a moment – is it possible that God chose you to experience a thorn for this very purpose? Because He knew you would boast in your weaknesses so that the power of Christ could dwell in you?

Whatever it is that you are going through, know this: God will see you through. It's not always easy, and I am still learning this myself. Trusting God is the most important thing you can do. We need to believe that He has our lives all planned out. It can be hard to comprehend this, but God has told us that we must trust Him anyway. Proverbs 3:5-6 says, "Trust in the LORD with all your heart and do not lean on your own understanding. In all your ways acknowledge Him, and He will make your paths straight" (NASB). Not only should we trust in God, but we should also have confidence that He will direct our paths when we don't know where to go.

As you can imagine, it was hard for my parents to trust in God, but they did. They believed that God would have a plan and a purpose for me. Life is not easy. It's not easy for me, and it won't be easy for you. God never says that life will be easy, but He does say He will be with us when tough times come.

There are times, even for me, when it feels like God is far away and He isn't there for me. There could be times when you feel like that as well, and that's okay. The great thing about God is that He is with us in every situation, whether we feel like it or not. He knows the difficulties, pains, trials, and burdens we carry. When we know God, we can give all these things over to Him, and He will carry them for us. Why? Because He cares for us. He loves us, and He wants to be there for us, through the good and the bad, through the valleys and the mountaintops.

My parents are an example of God's faithfulness in an incredibly difficult situation. Life was challenging for them, especially as they watched me go through all my struggles, knowing there were even more to come. My parents had to see their son go through operation after operation. They saw me prodded with needles and hospitalized for days at a time. I spent time in the operating room and the ICU for hours on end. It certainly wasn't easy for my parents. It was probably terrifying for both of them. However, when it came down to it, my parents didn't trust in man. They didn't trust the doctors. They trusted God.

When I was still a baby at Jamaica Hospital in Jamaica, NY, a nurse came into my mother's room and told her that doctors were doing operations on babies like me at Columbia Presbyterian Hospital in the Bronx. My parents decided to take me there. The doctors at Columbia Presbyterian gave my parents a glimpse of hope, which was far more than they had received at Jamaica Hospital. Instead of telling my parents that I would eventually become brain dead, these doctors advised them about an operation that might help. If the surgeons opened my skull and allowed my brain to grow, I would survive. Even so, I would have to undergo many operations and experience a lot of difficulties.

My parents agreed to this. They allowed me to go through one of the most challenging and life-changing surgeries of my life when I was only six weeks old. However, my parents prayed by faith. They believed that God had His hands on the doctors, as well as on me, during the operation.

This surgery was probably one of my longest to date. Afterward, I was in the NICU (Neonatal Intensive Care Unit) for about ten days. Thankfully, in the end, God brought me through and I survived.

Have you ever gone through something dramatic and wondered why you made it? Maybe it was a car accident, a house fire, cancer, a shooting, or an earthquake.

Think of it this way: is it possible that God has something greater in store for your life?

Several years ago, I was in a car accident and totaled the car. The front end was totally smashed in so that the car was no longer drivable. Even so, I jumped out of that car with no scratches, no broken bones, no injuries at all. About a year later, this same exact thing happened. I am so grateful that God protected me from both of these accidents. They were both my fault, and yet He kept me safe. I believe that God protected me because He isn't done with me yet. Is it possible that you, too, have survived your difficulties because God isn't done with you?

I bet that if I were to ask a doctor what was the likelihood of surviving sixty-eight operations, the probability would be very small. I have talked to people in the medical field, and they are always shocked when I tell them what I have endured. I even had one woman tell me, "You went through all that, and here you are, smiling." I am not smiling because of everything that has happened in my life but because I know I have God living inside me. I can't let the bad days outnumber the good days. That's what so many people do – they focus on the bad things that happen to them and don't see the good.

We will all go through bad things in our lives. Most of the time, however, the good will outweigh the bad. If this isn't true for you, ask yourself why. Find out what you're doing wrong that is causing you so much negativity. What do you have to change in your life so that you can have more good days?

Could it be that you should be spending more time with positive people who have a close relationship with Christ? Would it help to do a devotional or read the Bible? Sometimes, in order to have a good day, we have to change our mindset to remember that life is good. Even though I have experienced a lot of bad things, I have to remember that the good things in my life have always outweighed the bad, regardless of the situation.

Remember, even as Christians, life is not easy. There will be difficult times and situations. Even so, no matter what, God loves us. God has something great in store for our lives. If you are reading this and are a Christian, know this – God loves you. He cares for you and is there for you in all circumstances. In our lives, we have to take a step of faith and believe that good days will come. And if you're not a Christian, know this – God still loves you, and He wants you to come to a saving knowledge of Jesus by trusting and believing in Him.

I have known people who have been through much worse than I have, and they've survived. Why? Because God has a plan and a purpose for their lives. In Jeremiah 29:11, God says, "'For I know the plans I have for you,' declares the LORD, 'plans to prosper you and not to harm you, plans to give you a hope and a future.'" Not only does God have a plan and a purpose for your life, but He also has greater things in store for you than you can ever imagine. Know this today: God loves you, and He cares for you.

Let's go back to my story for a minute. From six

weeks to five years old, I underwent approximately seven operations that all lasted several hours at a time. The operations I had at Columbia Presbyterian were mostly for my hands. My doctors had to separate my fingers on my hands, and because of the way they did it, I only have nine fingers – five on my left hand and four on my right. Even so, I'm still able to hold a pen, write, do push-ups, lift weights, and hold hands. I'm not sure why I only have four fingers on my right hand. Maybe they couldn't find enough bone to create another finger, or maybe I didn't have enough skin graft from other parts of my body. Either way, I live with it and do pretty well with only nine fingers.

To this day, because I have very tiny veins, it is extremely difficult for phlebotomists to draw blood from me. Sometimes, it can take two or three pricking attempts before they can get blood from my arms. Usually, they have to resort to a butterfly needle because of how small my veins are. This has always been painful and frustrating for me, but God has given me the strength to bear it.

My facial surgeries were done at New York University with Dr. McCarthy and the staff of doctors there. If I had to choose which of my surgeries were the hardest, I would have to say they were the ones on my face. They were always terribly painful, and my face and eyes would get very swollen.

As I got older, I had to get my mouth rewired because of the way the doctors had to reshape and move my face forward. If you have ever experienced this, you know it's not an easy or pleasant experience. However, if you know me, then you know I don't like to do anything the easy way. Not only did I have my mouth rewired that time – I had it done twice.

I want to tell you today that, regardless of how you feel about yourself, if you're a woman, God thinks you're beautiful. If you're a man, God thinks you're handsome. We get so tied up in what other people think of us that we forget about what God thinks. I have done that as well. I used to worry about whether or not I was good-looking. Would I find the woman of God that He has for me? As I grew up, I started to learn that God had made me into His masterpiece. Regardless of other people's opinions, I needed to realize that the only thing that really mattered was what God thought.

There have been times in my life when I haven't been able to do everything the way others can, but God still believes I'm amazing. I've had to hold tight to that truth my entire life.

When I had my jaw wired, my mom had to make smoothies or other food that was soft enough for me to eat. It was also tough for me to speak with my jaw wired, so that was very emotional for me. Also, it seemed as if my hand was always in a cast. Because my hands were shortened and fused together when I was born, they are not as functional as normal hands. I can't raise or turn my hands over the way other people can.

I can remember going to get checkups at Columbia

Presbyterian and not knowing what to expect when the doctors took the bandages off my hands. What would my fingers look like? Would I be able to use them better than I could before? Because of how my hands and arms were, I could not maneuver them like other people. Therefore, it was difficult and painful for the doctors to look at my fingers. Eventually, the doctors got to know me quite well. They knew what they had to do, so when I walked in, they would get busy with taking an x-ray or removing stitches from my fingers. When I had to go for x-rays or other types of examinations, it would take several minutes for the technicians to figure out how to get my hands correctly situated for the test.

I can also remember one time when I had gotten an operation on my forehead. Because of the way the doctors did the operation, they had to make an opening in my skull from my right ear to my left ear. In order to do this, they had to cut off my hair. This particular time, I looked in the mirror and started to cry. I didn't think my hair was going to grow back. But regardless of what I looked like – hair or no hair, operation or no operation – I knew that God had created me, and He loved me. I am very thankful for parents who loved me, as well.

Recently, I asked my dad what was the most difficult situation from my first three years of life. He replied that they struggled to have the finances to come and see me at the hospital. He had to travel from Queens to Manhattan anytime he wanted to visit. How awesome is it that God provided each time, making it possible for my dad to see me? He is a great God!

My mom, however, was always able to stay with me while I was in the hospital, no matter how long I had to be there. She slept on a cot next to me, or in an empty bed, or, if need be, on the floor. One time, I was particularly nervous, so my mom came into the operating room with me. The doctor asked her to hold the mask over my face to put me to sleep. Every time she stayed with me before my operations, she did it for my comfort, so that I would have a little sense of peace that she was there with me. Even with all the machines beeping and nurses putting wires on me or trying to find a vein to put the IV in, my mom would stand in the room, waiting for me to fall asleep.

Before each operation, we would pray and sing the old hymn "Because He Lives." I like that hymn. It says:

> "Because He lives, I can face tomorrow.
> Because He lives, all fear is gone.
> Because I know He holds the future
> And life is worth the living
> Just because He lives."

I knew God held the future and that He was there, holding me, even though there were times I was afraid. I didn't always believe that I would survive. Sometimes, I wondered if I would see the next day. I wondered what the future was going to hold for me. We had some interesting times at the hospital, but in God's miraculous ways, I never flatlined and I never had to be brought back to life. Praise the Lord!

2

THE REAL WORLD

Five years after the doctors told my parents that I wouldn't survive, my parents saw me enter the Henry Viscardi School. This was a specific school for people with disabilities ranging from pre-k to high school. I started going to this school in kindergarten and basically grew up attending there. I rode the bus like everyone else. We would go on field trips, play sports, and have swim classes. My mom told me that for the first few weeks of swim classes, I wouldn't go in the water. However, I finally did, and if the instructors had kept me there, I probably wouldn't have gotten out.

Going to a school for people with disabilities wasn't easy. Even though all the other students had disabilities, too, they would still make fun of me. They called me "monster" and "freak," just like the kids in my neighborhood and other places. Even though it hurt at times, I tried not to get angry or say mean things back to those who insulted me.

But the difficulties didn't end with being picked on. Time and time again, I saw my friends and others in the school pass away due to complications with their disabilities.

There was one kid on my bus who would say mean things to me. I did my best to ignore him and anyone else who would make the occasional snide remark. Eventually, this kid and I ended up on the same hockey team together. I found out he wasn't so bad after all. He eventually ended up passing away, and I had to speak at his memorial service. I remember giving his mother his hockey stick. We were both emotional, knowing that we would never see him again. Even though this kid had a history of making fun of me, we had become friends because of being on the same team. This just goes to show that sometimes, things happen that we do not expect. In time, much can change.

When you're living with a disability, it is hard to see the people around you passing away. Some of them were people I knew, and some I didn't. Some were adults, and others were teenagers. Watching all of this happen, it was hard not to think to myself, *Am I next? Am I going to be the next one who is announced on the loudspeaker to the whole school?*

My parents were told I wouldn't make it to my eighteenth birthday, and yet, here I am, more than double that. I am still alive, and all I can say is that it's all God. Only God knows how long we will live. Ecclesiastes 3:2 says, "[There is] a time to give birth and a time to die;

a time to plant and a time to uproot what is planted" (NASB). We do not know what's going to happen from one day to the next. We could be here today and gone tomorrow. We don't always fully understand why tragedies happen, but as Christians, we know that God will work everything out for our good and His glory.

Like the kid on the bus, there were others who made fun of me. Even some adults would make assumptions about me that were untrue and hurtful. For example, the first time I had a seizure, one of the nurses thought I was a girl. It may have been because I had curly hair when I was a child. Even now, sometimes people think I have a woman's name or voice when I speak to them over the phone. Figure that one out.

Another time, the youth pastor and senior pastor came to visit me in the hospital. My mom asked the youth pastor why he hadn't invited me to come and be a part of the youth group. His response was that he thought I was retarded. Regardless of this statement, I still wanted to go to youth group when I could. The teenagers who went always treated me well and welcomed me to the meetings without question. They allowed me to participate in the games they were playing, including basketball. Of course, I wasn't the top-picked player everyone wanted on their teams, whether it was in my neighborhood, at youth events, or in school. I couldn't shoot the basketball that well because of my shortened arms, and I didn't have much strength, so I didn't always do well. But I always tried my best and had fun.

However, in contrast to the people who said hurtful things about me, my parents always treated me as if I didn't have a disability from the time I was small. They treated me like a normal person. They didn't hold me back from what I wanted to try or do. I wasn't a person who wanted to give up, and I never raised the white flag of surrender. I'm grateful for parents who allowed me that freedom. They didn't put me in a box and say, "Well, he's not going to be able to do a lot, so we will just limit him to only what we think he will be able to do." That's definitely not what they did, and I'm thankful for that. I wonder what would have happened if they did. Where would I be today? What would have become of me if my parents had truly limited me?

I also have two sisters named Judy and Susan. There is a significant age difference between the three of us. My oldest sister, Judy, was twenty-one when I was born. Susan was sixteen, so she still lived at home for a few years until she went off and got married.

The great thing about my relationship with my sisters was that they have always cared for me as a younger brother. Just like my parents, my sisters don't look down on me or think of me any differently because of my disability. When they had children, it was the same way. We would all hang out and play sports together. I was able to enjoy parties and holiday events at their houses. Several years ago, however, my family suffered our most difficult experience yet – we lost my sister, Susan. It was tough. We know things like this happen in our lives, but we don't always understand why.

There are times in our lives when we feel like we are in a fight for our lives. Or maybe we feel like we're in a boxing match, like Rocky fighting the Russian. I believe we have all felt trapped, like a boxer who puts his opponent in a corner and beats on him until he wants to give up. The devil, our enemy, does the same thing to us. He wants us to surrender. Even so, we can't give the enemy that victory. Just because a boxer is laying down on the mat doesn't mean he is finished. It doesn't mean he is down for the count. Like the boxer, we need to get back up, believing that God has greater things in store for us, regardless of what we go through, regardless of the thorns in our lives or the weaknesses we suffer. There were times in my life when I felt beaten. I was struck down and wanted to give up. However, with God's strength, I was never destroyed. 2 Corinthians 4:8-9 (NASB) says, "We are afflicted in every way, but not crushed; perplexed, but not despairing; persecuted, but not forsaken; struck down, but not destroyed."

I never allowed my disability to stop me from doing what I wanted to do. For instance, I was very involved in sports. When I was five years old, the founder of a baseball and bowling league called "We Try Harder" came to my school and introduced himself to us. I started playing with this league that year and stayed in it until I got out of high school. A lot of my teammates were also students at my school. It was fun because this league had both children and teenagers with disabilities. We also had people on the team who didn't have disabilities.

My parents allowed me to play in this league. However, the league had set up limitations so myself and the other players wouldn't get hurt. For example, we would use plastic and metal bats depending on who was batting. We also adapted some of the rules to make sure that no one got seriously injured. We always used tennis balls as well instead of using regular baseballs. I loved sports, but I had to figure out what I could and couldn't do. It turns out that the word "couldn't" wasn't in my vocabulary. For that, I am grateful.

It was a great experience to be in a baseball league and bowling team. I was pretty good at the sports I played, even though I had to use some different equipment. My bowling ball was different from everyone else's. The ball was the normal size, but did not have any holes in it. I would just put it in the palm of my hand, spin it, and hit the pins. The highest score I ever got up to this point was a 202. I can also remember that I played several different positions on the baseball team, but my favorite position was pitcher because pitchers always seem to win the game for the team.

As I got older, I was also able to play football. I used to play in the streets with my friends, and I eventually became a Denver Broncos fan. A lot of people have asked me why I chose the Broncos as my team. Honestly, I don't know. I think I was watching a game one time with my Uncle Dorsey, one of my namesakes, and the Broncos were one of the teams playing at the time.

Regardless of the trials, frustrations, and distresses

in my life, I have always tried to be confident and do my best in everything. I never wanted anything to stop me from trying something new, even if it was just one time. Some things I tried include ice skating, water and snow tubing, skiing, and white-water rafting. I may have needed a little help with these activities, but I made it. I have even tried driving a jet ski, which I didn't think I would be able to do because of my hands – but I could! The second time I went on a jet ski, however, I hit my head on the handlebars and bruised my nose pretty badly. Thankfully, I didn't break it. I also went to amusement parks and rode roller coasters. Once, I went with my dad on a spinning ride that came apart while we were on it and went spinning down the parking lot! Thankfully, we were able to get out of the ride with no serious injuries.

You would think that because my fingers are small and I can't lift my hands above my head, I wouldn't want to even try indoor mountain climbing, but I did. I didn't care that I might not be able to do it – I wanted to try. I was living in the real world, and as much as possible, I wanted to be treated as a normal person.

I say all this to encourage you. Just tell yourself, "If Dorsey can do something like this with his disability, so can I!" If I failed, at least I tried. Sometimes I would even try these things a second time, just to see what would happen.

One of the great things about my dad is that he has always been willing to support me and encourage me in what God wants me to do. Every time I've said, "Dad, I want to do this," he would say, "Hey, if you want to try it, go ahead. It's up to you." That is something I want to encourage you with. If you feel that you want to do something and you're afraid, first pray about it and see what God would have you to do. If you feel a release to do it, then do it. The worst thing that can happen is that you fail, which we all do sometimes in our lives.

Eventually, I realized there were some things I really wasn't able to do, but to be honest, there wasn't much. One of the most significant things I can't do is lift my hands above my head. This limits me from getting things off high shelves or extending my arms full-length. That's about all I can't do. Doctors told me that I would need braces to walk because of my fused toes, and to this day, I have never worn any braces. I try to keep my body healthy by going to the gym, although I have to admit that I sometimes slack off. Even so, I still try to push myself to go.

At one point when I was young, I realized that I was one of the most fortunate students at my school. Why? Because of all the students I went to school with, I was probably one of the few whose father was still at home or whose parents hadn't divorced. I was able to walk and breathe on my own. I could run, I could talk, and I could do most of the other things normal people do, even if I did have some limitations.

I remember that one day, I asked my mom if I was adopted. I could not understand how I became so fortunate. How in the world did I go through all that I went through and still have both of my birth parents? Not only did I have to go through all of it, but they did, too! How did that happen? My parents didn't care that I had a birth defect. They didn't care that I would face many challenges and have to go through operations. They weren't even concerned about the fact that I might not survive. They cared for me enough to say, "Okay, God. We will take care of this child You have given to us. We will love him no matter what happens and no matter what we go through."

Isn't it just like our Heavenly Father and what He does for us? He loves us regardless of what we have done in our lives.

When I got older, my mom told me that in kindergarten, I thought I was the normal one and that it was the other kids who were different. I didn't realize I was one of the different kids. Even as an adult, I don't always feel like I'm different, even though I know I am. I live in the real world, and I realize these things. However, I also realize that I am a masterpiece. I am God's perfect creation.

As I have learned more about Apert Syndrome, I have met others who also have it, and there are different forms. I know that God molded and shaped me, knowing exactly what I would have to go through, but I still ask myself, "Why did God make me this way? Why did He make others with different severities of Apert?"

I have a great, theological answer to that question. I don't know.

Psalm 139:13-16 says:

> For You formed my inward parts; You wove me together in my mother's womb. I will give thanks to You, for I am fearfully and wonderfully made; wonderful are Your works, and my soul knows it very well. My frame was not hidden from You, when I was made in secret, and skillfully wrought in the depths of the earth; Your eyes have seen my unformed substance; and in Your book were all written the days that were ordained for me, when as yet there was not one of them. (NASB)

I've had people say to me, "Well, if you believe you are God's masterpiece, why did you decide to go through all of those operations?" My answer has several parts. First, I didn't realize that I was God's masterpiece when I was younger. It wasn't until later in life that I understood that He allowed this to happen for His plan and purpose. Additionally, the operations helped me to survive. If it weren't for those operations, I wouldn't be here today. I also wanted to look better so that I could fit in and be accepted. However, even though I had the operations, I was still teased and pointed at.

If I hadn't had the operations, is it possible that I wouldn't have gotten made fun of so much?

Probably not, because people can be cruel and mean. It's also possible that without these operations, I would have had a tougher time in my own life. I would have had more questions about what I was able to accomplish. Like anything in life, I won't know until I see God face to face and ask Him what would've happened if I hadn't gotten the operations. However, I've never regretted having any one of them.

As another result of Apert, I have a speech impediment. It was a lot worse when I was younger than it is now. People had a hard time understanding me. My school had speech therapists who helped students like me. I had to go to the therapists through most of my schooling. I liked some things about it, but sometimes I dreaded having to go through those challenges again and again. A lot of what the therapists gave me to do just didn't make sense. For example, they would have me look at different clothing magazines, and I couldn't help but wonder, "Why am I doing this?" Even so, I went. It was difficult and frustrating at times. Now I'm glad I did, because it improved my speech, although it is not and may never be perfect.

Even now, I have had people think that when I call them, it is a prank call, or they have a hard time understanding me when I leave a message on the answering machine. Just as I can relate to Paul with his thorn in the flesh, I can also relate to Moses, who had a stuttering problem. It may be different, but there are certainly similarities, as well. Why? Because Moses thought that his stuttering issue would disqualify him from the calling God had on his life.

Exodus 4:10-12 (NASB) says, "Then Moses said to

the LORD, 'Please, Lord, I have never been eloquent, neither recently nor in time past, nor since You have spoken to Your servant; for I am slow of speech and slow of tongue.' The LORD said to him, 'Who has made man's mouth? Or who makes him mute or deaf, or seeing or blind? Is it not I, the LORD? Now then go, and I, even I, will be with your mouth, and teach you what you are to say.'"

In the verses that follow this passage, Moses tells God that he wants Him to send someone else. He lacked the self-confidence to think that he could do anything for God. But look at what tremendous things God did through Moses! We need to realize that regardless of who we are, God can use us.

Sometimes, when we are born with birth defects or experience disabilities later in life, we wonder if we'll ever be able to get back to where we were before. We wonder if we'll ever be able to improve our walking abilities, our speech impairments, or our health in general. We don't know unless we take that step and go through the process of rehabilitation or therapy to see where God will take us.

Now, I say that I knew God had a purpose for my life because that's what His Word says. The question is, did I always believe that? Did I always accept the Bible as truth? I can honestly say I don't think I did. There were times when I questioned if God had a plan, and if He did, what it was. However, I knew my family loved and accepted me. I don't know where I would be without them, especially my mom and dad. They were the ones who always surrounded and comforted me through the storms of life.

I'm glad that God knows everything. As long as God lives, which is forever, any fears we have can be removed because He holds the future. We don't know what we are going to face, but God does. He has seen everything that we have encountered, and He will see everything we face in the future. Since God knows everything we go through even before we do, He knew the doctors would tell my parents I would be a vegetable. He knew they would be encouraged to put me in an institution, too. He knew I would face kids who picked on me and that I would have adults say untrue or inaccurate things about me. But regardless of what people said about me, I believed that God knew the truth of what would happen to me. He loved me enough to see me through these situations in my life.

As you can see, I wanted to be just like everyone else. But as with any type of disability, I still realize that at times, I am not.

3

RUN THE RACE

"Do you not know that those who run in a race all run, but only one receives the prize? Run in such a way that you may win." (1 Corinthians 9:24)

Growing up, I was involved in the Olympic games that are held for people with disabilities. I especially liked doing the track events, like the 100m and the 200m, because they reminded me that I also had to continue running the race of life. In addition to track, I did the 50m in swimming and some field events, such as the obstacle course.

There's something that we need to learn – life is not a sprint, but a marathon. Sometimes, it's going to be an uphill race, and it's going to be hard. Your physical body will feel like it's burning and your legs will get weak until you get to the top of the hill, where you can get some rest. Then you're not going to have to push as hard anymore. Once you reach the top, you can relax. You're still going to have to run, but it's not going to be as hard.

That's how life will feel to you. That's how life has felt to me at times.

When I was younger, I was able to ride a bicycle. I remember that one time I was riding down a friend's driveway, and I didn't realize a car was coming down the street. I had to slide, and I landed pretty close to the car. That was scary. Another time, I was playing baseball in the street, and I got hit in the head with a metal baseball bat. Then, in gym class once, I bounced off one of my classmates, fell, and broke my arm. I injured myself in the same way again in college, though that time I was just clumsy and fell up the stairs while I was walking into a building. My friend Brock told me I would be okay, and I believed him. I didn't think to get my arm checked. Over the weekend, I was playing different games, and my injury didn't hurt. However, on Monday, my arm was swollen. I walked into my friend Doug's room and said, "I don't think this is normal." Doug and I went to the hospital, where I found out my arm was so badly broken that I had to get an operation to put it back into place. I stayed on campus and only had to take a little time off from school. It took approximately six weeks for me to get the cast off, but eventually I was able to go back to class.

This is all a part of running the race we call life. When something bad happens, you get back up – even if it requires surgery for a broken arm. Regardless of what I have faced, whether in my physical or spiritual life, I have always known that I need to push forward.

I couldn't allow anything to stop me from doing what God wanted to do in my life. I couldn't allow what other people said to stop me from doing what I wanted to accomplish. I wanted to show others that I could turn around their insults and say, "Yes, I can." You can do the same thing. When people tell you that you are not going to be able to do something, you can say, "Yes, I can."

Since I was brought up in a Christian home, I tried my best to go to church as often as I could. However, that wasn't always possible, whether it was because of my operations, being in the hospital, or involvement with sports. There were times in my life when I felt close to God, and there were times I felt as though He was far away. I soon learned that we all feel that way at times in our lives. That is normal. However, I had to realize that regardless of where I feel God is, He is actually always there for us.

When you're preparing for the Olympics, you have to train. You need to run with weights to make your muscles stronger. But then, once it's time for you to run the race, you have to take off the weights. If you try to run with them on, they will hold you back from running at full speed. It's the same with the spiritual race we are all running. The weights that we have in our lives hold us back from effectively doing what God has for us. We need to let go of our weights so that we can run freely to God with nothing holding us back from what He has for us.

What are weights? Weights can be the physical things that we put on our bodies for training. Or, they can be something that is holding us back from serving God, such as fear, doubt, insecurity, or pain from the past. There are sometimes even sins that hold us back from receiving the fullness of what God has for us. That is why we need to break the chains of the weights we are carrying and run full on.

One of my favorite songs is called "Break Every Chain" by Tasha Cobbs Leonard.

The chorus of the song goes:

> "There is power in the name of Jesus
> To break every chain
> Break every chain
> Break every chain."

God wants to break every chain that is holding us back from what He has for us. In my life, the chains were fears, doubts, worries, and concerns. I wouldn't be where I am today if I had not been able to get rid of all the hurts, pains, disappointments, and struggles. I would still be held down, and I would be hindered from realizing what God has for me. Eventually, little by little, God has broken those chains in my life. He can do the same thing for you, as well.

Philippians 4:13 (NASB) says, "I can do all things through Him who strengthens me." It's important to mention that this does not mean that God will give us the strength to do absolutely anything. For example, if we try to lift a 1,000-pound rock, God is not going to miraculously enable us to pick it up. I have lost many races, and I've lost many sports games. Does this mean that God didn't give me the strength to win? No, not at all. It's up to God to allow us to do what He has for us, according to His will.

What this Scripture is telling us is that the strength that we get for life does not come from an outside source but from Christ Himself. I can tell you that there have been times when I have felt weak. However, God gave me the strength to keep going, to keep getting up each morning, and to keep moving forward. God says with Him, all things are possible. As I realized that I could do all things through Christ who gives me strength, I began to be content with my circumstances. I eventually became happy living with my disability. I do not want to live the type of life where I think about my limitations all the time. I do not want to tell myself there is something I can't do. However, even though I say I do not have any limitations, I have learned to be okay with the ones I know I do have.

Throughout my life, and even now, I have needed to learn that the weights we have to carry are sometimes difficult to deal with. The Bible talks about these weights as the sins that we deal with. When we let go of those sins (or weights), it's easier to run the race of life. We need to give those weights back to Jesus. We need to place them at His feet. We need to fix our eyes on Him and say, "God, I know that with You, I can do all things, because You give me strength."

And then we need to ask Him to help us to continue this race that we call life.

4

THE BATTLES
I FOUGHT

As a teenager, I often thought about what I wanted to do when I got older. I went from wanting to be a nurse to wanting to be a baseball player (typical boy), to wanting to work with computers or be a lifeguard. I never pursued the last one. I wasn't that fast, so I knew I would never be able to make the swim to save someone.

I also thought about relationships and dating. Even with a disability, I liked talking to the girls at youth group or school. Sometimes, when I would look in the mirror, I would wonder how some of the pretty girls would want to talk to me. I asked myself if they would be interested in a guy like me because of my appearance. I sometimes felt that I wasn't a good-looking guy. I hadn't yet learned that what really mattered was what was on the inside, not just beauty on the outside.

Life was hard for me, and at times, it still is. There

were times when I wondered if I would make it. I even wondered if I would consider suicide. It wasn't that I didn't want to live; it was that the enemy, the devil, was pushing buttons in the back of my head. Now, granted, these weren't literal buttons. They were thoughts I would get in my mind. The devil was the one who would whisper to me that I should just give up on life because it wasn't going to work out. He told me that my dreams and God's plans would never come to pass. The enemy made me believe I wouldn't make it through college, I wouldn't find a ministry opportunity, and I wouldn't find the wife God has for me. He said God didn't have a purpose for my life. He'd whisper that I wasn't going to accomplish anything and that I was a loser, and there was nothing I could do about it.

We all have those buttons, those little things the enemy tells us we can't do. He says that we won't be able to go to college, that we won't get that job we just interviewed for, or that we won't get married. If you're already married, he'll tell you that your marriage won't survive. Sometimes, we start believing those lies, and then we begin to give up on the life God has given us.

Why do we listen to the enemy?

Instead of paying attention to the devil, we need to put him in his place. We need to realize that he is the liar of liars and that God does, in fact, have something great in store for our lives. When I was thinking about killing myself and ending my life, I still knew God was there with me, even though I didn't always feel Him.

Even when I wondered what His plans or purposes were for my life, the biggest issue was just that I couldn't see those things in the moment. That doesn't mean they didn't exist.

As I was enduring all these trials, one day my pastor asked if there was anyone in the church who wanted to accept Christ as Lord and Savior. I was the only person who went up to the altar that day. I raised my hands and gave my heart to Christ, saying I wanted Him to be a part of my life. That doesn't mean that from that day forward, I was perfect, sinless, or free from mockery and trials. Just because our lives belong to Christ doesn't mean we won't face battles or get into a spiritual fight. We will. However, God will protect us. He will always be right there with us in that fight. If we read to the end of the Bible, we know that Christ has already ultimately won the war, even though we will still deal with battles daily in our lives.

John 10:10 (NASB) says, "The thief comes only to steal and kill and destroy; I came that they may have life, and have it abundantly." God wants us to have a life of abundance and joy, but that doesn't mean it will always happen that way. He also tells us that we will have trials and tribulations. However, He wants us to live life to the best that we can. Why? Because He has great things in store for us, not only in the here and now, but also in eternity. If we want to have the life of joy and happiness that God wants us to live, we cannot allow the enemy, the thief, to come and destroy us.

Regardless of the battles we fight, God does protect us. However, He also wants to see what we're going to do when the enemy attacks. He wants to know if we're going to run away or if we're going to run to Him.

Faith has played a big part in my life, and for good reason – it needed to. If I didn't have faith in God and in what I know He has for my life, I don't know what would have happened to me. We especially need faith when we are going through tough times. My faith and trust in God are the main reasons why I survived. I also always had a group of friends who were with me when times got tough. Yes, I had my family, and they were some of my greatest supporters. But sometimes we also need to have a group of friends who will be there to help, support, and pray for us.

At times, life may be different for me because I am living with a disability. However, for the most part, I'm the same as anyone else. I don't get an exemption from tough situations just because I'm a reverend with a disability. I wish I'd had the friends that I do now back when I was younger, because it probably would have helped me a lot more. Some of the amazing friends I have now are Kevin Bateman, Chris Goldyn, Pastor Dom, Adam Barnes, Dan Desrosiers, and Matt Bellomo. Not only do I have this support group of guys, but I also had guys that I would hang out with at church. When I talk to these guys, I realize that I am not alone in the boat. The struggles and battles that I have to deal with are the same struggles that they face, especially as guys.

In Exodus 17, the Israelites are battling the Amalekites. As long as Moses' arms are lifted, the Israelites are winning, but when he lowers his arms, the Amalekites gain strength. When Moses' arms get heavy, his friends Aaron and Hur hold them up for him. I encourage you to ask God to bring you Aarons and Hurs who will help you fight the battles in your life. If you feel alone, find friends who will support and encourage you. Find people of the same faith and age who will be there when you are down. You'll be able to do the same for them, as well. Specifically, my Aaron and Hur are my friends Chris Goldyn and Adam Barnes. I can always count on them to be with me. I can be honest with them about what I am facing, and they will encourage and pray with me.

5

FRIENDS

A long time ago, Christian music artist Michael W. Smith wrote a song called "Friends" for someone who was moving away. I don't think Michael realized how big of a song it would become and how much of an impact it would have on so many people. That song makes me realize that regardless of how far away my friends are, they will always be my friends. No matter how often we talk or see each other, our friendship will remain strong. Of course, I can only really say this about true friends – the ones who have stuck by me and have been there regardless of what I have gone through.

I had friends growing up who I liked to hang out with, go on bike rides with, or have over to my house to play GI Joe vs. Cobra for hours on end. We would go to the park down the block and play baseball, play football in the street, or even play with toy guns to see who could shoot each other first. I can remember some of those kids' names, like Joey, Michael, and Chichi, while other names have faded from my mind.

Like the friends I made as a child, sometimes our friends only last for a season in our lives. Sometimes, I wonder if some of them really were my friends or if they just spent time with me because they felt sorry about my disability. Or maybe they took advantage of me because I was the kid with all the toys – at least, that's what they led me to believe. However, I'm not saying I had a sad childhood, because I certainly did not. Sure, I had sad times just like everybody else, but the joy definitely overwhelmed the sadness.

Let me ask you this today: who are your true friends? Who are the friends you can call up at 2 o'clock in the morning to talk about what you are dealing with? Do you have that friend that you can call up and say, "Hey, I need someone to listen to me," without any judgment, any advice, or any correction at all? I think those types of friends are few and far between. Proverbs 18:24 (NASB) says, "A man of too many friends comes to ruin, but there is a friend who sticks closer than a brother." I don't know if this was really a prophecy about Jesus, but have you considered if Jesus is truly that one friend who sticks closer than a brother?

We may not always think of Jesus as a friend. We think of Him as God, Lord, and Savior, and those things are true. However, when Jesus was here on earth, He picked out twelve disciples, twelve men that He would walk around town with for the next three years. He never gave up on them, no matter what. He never called them unfaithful, never said they were useless, and never walked away when they committed a sin. Even when Peter denied Jesus, He still loved him. After His crucifixion, Jesus had one of His own disciples, Thomas, doubt Him. Thomas didn't believe that Jesus was alive, but when he finally saw Him, all Jesus said was, "Do not be unbelieving, but believing" (John 20:27 NASB).

That's the type of friend that I would want in my life – one who would always believe in me, always say, "I've got your back," and always be there to pull me out of the pit when I fall down. I have friends like this, and they are the ones I allow to speak into my life. They have permission to correct me, tell me when I'm wrong, or say when I'm making the wrong decision. Of course, I go to God first and foremost. Then, I'll ask my friends for their advice, listen, and decide from what God has told me whether or not I listen to my friends.

Jesus was with His disciples in John 15:12-17 (NASB) when He told them, "This is My commandment, that you love one another, just as I have loved you. Greater love has no one than this, that one lay down his life for his friends. You are My friends if you do what I command you. No longer do I call you slaves, for the slave does not know what his master is doing; but I have called you friends, for all things that I have heard from My Father I have made known to you. You did not choose Me but I chose you, and appointed you that you would go and bear fruit, and that your fruit would remain, so that whatever you ask of the Father in My name He may give to you. This I command you, that you love one another."

God clearly calls us to love one another, and love is one of the most foundational footholds of friendship that any of us can have. If we do not have love, we do not have anything. As 1 Corinthians 13 says, we sound like a noisy gong or a clanging cymbal if we do not have love. We need love in our lives – love for God, our friends, and our spouse.

Growing up, I had to learn what a true friend was. In my teenage years, I had friends in the youth group and even in my school. However, I do not hang out with most of these friends anymore. I can count on one hand how many friends from my teenage years I stay in contact with today. Life is difficult; it brings change. People go off and get married. Some stay single. Some have kids and jobs, and life eventually becomes busy. Sometimes we grow apart from old friends and grow close to new ones. Nevertheless, I'm very persistent, and I do try to keep in touch with my friends. I especially try to stay close to those that I know are there for me, love me, and will hold me up when I need them. I will do the same thing for them when they need me.

I hope that everyone who is reading this book has real, true friends who you can call up when you're excited for that new job, that new engagement, or that new baby. I also hope that those same friends will be there with you when your hearts are broken, when you're wondering what will happen next, or when you don't know what to do. The friends you trust the most will be there for you when you need to pour your heart out. I'm thankful to God that I have friends like these. I'm not alone in the battles of life, the difficulties I face, or the joys I celebrate.

> *Ecclesiastes 4:12 says, "Though one may be overpowered, two can defend themselves. A cord of three strands is not quickly broken." I hope you have close friends. But whether or not you do, remember that you have a truer friend than any other in Jesus. He will stick closer than a brother.*

Remember that today.

6

WAITING FOR THE ONE

When you've been told for years by bullies that you look like a monster, you start to wonder if anyone besides God and your family and friends will ever truly love you. Will a woman ever one day truly say, "Yes, I will be your girlfriend," or, "Yes, I will marry you"? Do you know for certain that these things will happen? I know I don't.

People often say to enjoy the single life because marriage is hard. But to be honest, being single isn't the easiest thing, either. It's definitely difficult to see your friends going off and getting married while you're still the single guy.

The only true girlfriend I've had was in junior high and high school. I had known her for most of my life, and we were together for approximately three years. Since we both had disabilities, our parents were always around us, and they'd have to come with us on all our dates. That was always interesting.

However, the more I read the Bible, the more I

realized that I had to be with someone who had the same beliefs that I had. This girlfriend was not a Christian, so we eventually broke up. Even after we stopped dating, though, we were still friends. We would still hang out at the mall, go to dinner, and occasionally even go to the movies. When we were in high school, we even ended up going to the prom together, and I took her sister the year after that. However, we did not think of these events as dates. Although this girl and I don't keep in touch as often anymore, I will always consider her the only girlfriend I had in high school.

When I was young, I was part of Forward Face, an organization and support group for those who had facial disfigurements. Each year, they had a Christmas banquet and dance. There was a young woman across the street from my church, and I would talk to her on occasion. One year, I decided to ask her if she would come with me to the event. She politely agreed. It was a great evening. We had dinner, danced, and met other people with craniofacial disabilities. Both of us had a great time; however, I never ended up asking this young lady to be my girlfriend.

Once I realized that I should be dating a Christian, I had a few crushes on girls in youth group. There was one girl in particular that I liked. Actually, all of the other guys did, too. We all knew it, and that made it kind of fun. Her father was an ex-Marine, and he was a big dude. He was also in the army, so I knew better than to hurt his daughter or step over the wrong line. As much as I would have liked to, this girl and I never dated or even went out together alone.

When we like someone, we often look at their outward appearance. That's just what people do. It's part of how we were created. God even says in 1 Samuel 16:7, "Man looks at the outward appearance, but the LORD looks at the heart" (NASB).

I want to do what God does by looking at the heart of the person I am with. I want to make sure that she loves God and has a strong relationship with Him. That doesn't mean I always look at the heart first. I should, but I don't. Men are often first attracted to a woman by her outward appearance. They don't tend to look at what she is like inside – who she is, what she likes to do for fun, and most importantly, whether or not she is a Christ-follower. It's normal to do this. We all do, myself included. However, because we usually first look at the outside of a person, sometimes I wonder if girls will be attracted to me because I have a disability and don't look like everyone else. I've said this before, and I'll say it again: I've always tried to think of myself as someone who is normal, but when I look in the mirror, I realize that I am different.

That's when I have to remind myself that I was created in the image of God and that, in His eyes, I am perfect. In His plan, He has something great in store for me, no matter what happens. I hope and pray that when I meet ladies I like, they will get to know me by looking at my heart. I want to do the same thing for them. I want to see them, not for their outward appearance, but for their passion, desire, and love for God. I want to see what God has for them and what His plans and purposes are for their lives. I want to see their passion for worshiping God and their desire to pray to Him. I want to love them for their desire to get to know God more and more, and I want to see how much they want to do God's work.

As I said earlier, we all have to be attracted to the man or woman we want to date. However, even more than that, I want God to teach me that just because a person is attractive on the outside, that doesn't mean they are attractive on the inside.

Let me give you an example. Let's say I want to buy a 2020 BMW M4 that can reach 190 mph. Let's say it can go from 0 to 60 in 3.8 seconds. However, when I get it home and drive it for the first time, I realize that the motor is shot. It's no good, and the motor will have to be replaced. On the other hand, let's say I could buy an old jalopy that has a great engine, can go over 200 miles per hour, and will last me for many years. Which one would you want to have? Personally, I would rather have the car that looks like a jalopy but has a great engine, rather than the car that is great on the outside, but has an engine that's useless.

Again, it's not about the outside appearance. The inside is what counts to God.

I have had crushes and interests in my adult life, but though I've had good friendships with women, I haven't had a girlfriend since high school. One of the reasons is that whenever I ask someone out or see if she is interested in being my girlfriend, she ends up just wanting to be friends. I think the other reason is that I've been hurt before when women have turned me down, so I'm worried about that happening again.

It's not easy waiting for the woman of God that He has for me. I have read countless books and heard many sermons on dating and relationships. If there's one thing I've learned, it's that when you want to be more than friends with a girl, you have to be patient. You can't force it when it comes to relationships. I have done that, and it doesn't help anything. It's important to build a friendship with the other person first. That way, you can see where that friendship goes. Also, as the guy, you have to ask the girl out; you never know what might happen. So just ask! If the girl says no, then at least you know. Unfortunately, "no's" are a part of life.

When I was in Bible college, I went to a special chapel service each semester that focused on dating. I always hoped to get some ideas or advice on how to do things better. It was a great chapel service, and I took plenty of notes and learned a lot. However, even though I met a lot of friends on campus, no relationships worked out. There was this special code at the college: a ring by spring, or your money back. I knew that "ring by spring" was just a joke to make people laugh and wasn't totally accurate, so I wasn't really bothered that it didn't happen for me. There were a few girls that I liked, and I wish I could've dated them. But I didn't, and it was all in God's plan. It's a hard lesson to learn, but sometimes the timing we imagine doesn't match the timing of God's will. We need to learn to trust Him in that.

I went through the same things as everyone else. I was single, but wanted a girlfriend and eventually a wife. There I was, the single guy. I wanted to have a wedding date, but always seemed to be the guy without a date. Nothing stopped me from asking girls out, but when I had built up a good enough friendship with someone to ask her to be my girlfriend, I usually got rejected. That stung sometimes. I've often wondered what it was about me that made those girls not want to be more than friends. There were times when I wondered if they declined because of my looks. However, I still opted to take the risk and ask instead of staying silent and regretting it later. The worst thing girls can say is no, right? I haven't let the rejections of the past stop me from asking again. I've learned that you have to take risks, because if you don't, you'll never know what could have happened.

To this day, I am still waiting for the woman God wants me to be with. Unlike Paul, I am definitely not called to live the single life.

My friend Chris Goldyn tries to tell me that I may be single for the rest of my life. That is a possibility, since God never tells us with certainty that we will get married. However, His Word says that He doesn't want man to be alone. I wish that was a promise, and I hope that someday I will find my own special someone. Do I believe there is only one person out there for each of us? No, absolutely not. That would be like looking for a needle in a haystack. However, I do think that God will show us who it is that He wants us to be with. I've talked to many of my guy friends who are either married or are currently dating the girl of their dreams. I've heard a lot of stories from them about how difficult relationships and marriage can be. When they tell me these things, I can't help but think to myself that maybe it's better I'm still single.

Although I haven't been in a relationship since high school, I am sure that dating and marriage are not easy. Regardless of the woman God sends me, I am sure there will be challenges, and whether or not I get married, I am okay with God's will. On the one hand, if I don't get married, I will probably always hope to have that opportunity. On the other hand, if I am destined to stay single, I will try to live my life to the full extent of the happiness that God has for me.

7

LEARNING GOD'S PURPOSE

As you can see, I have been through a lot in my life. I have also asked a lot of questions. One of the questions I asked God was why would He allow me to be born this way? What purpose would God have for me to go through all these struggles, obstacles, and trials? Even though I've endured a lot, I know God allowed it to happen for a purpose. As I've grown up and started to develop a better relationship with God, I've begun to recognize what that purpose is. I believe that God wants to use my disability to inspire and encourage other people. Perhaps He wants me to help others realize that they can do anything God has for them, regardless of what limitations they might have.

God knew He was placing me in a family that would love me, care for me, and support me, just like they did for all their other children. My parents never really cared that their son had a disability. They were not ashamed to take me out in public, and the most important place they took me was church.

I may not fully know God's plan and purpose for making me the way He did until I see Him face to face. However, I know that, even though my life isn't easy, God had a great reason for creating me the way He did. When I read Romans 8:28, I am reminded, "And we know that God causes all things to work together for good to those who love God, to those who are called according to His purpose" (NASB). I sometimes wonder why anyone would call what I'm going through "good." It's not always easy to figure out the answers to questions like that, but when we love God and are living in His purpose, He will work out all that we go through for good.

Every day, we hear about devastating tragedies that happen in the world we live in, but we can have confidence that when we are living for God, He will work all of these things out for good. Have you ever gotten laid off from a job? Or perhaps you've been dating someone for a while, and you're starting to think about popping the question when your boyfriend or girlfriend suddenly breaks off the relationship. You're upset and depressed, right? However, six months down the road, you find a better job and meet someone new who treats you much better than your ex did. In both cases, you look back and understand why everything happened the way it did.

There have been plenty of times in my life when I've

wondered why God would allow me to go through all that I have experienced. Was being teased and having sixty-eight operations easy? Was being picked, prodded, and poked more times than I can count a good time? No! However, God says He works everything out for His glory and our good. Not some things. Not certain things. Not a few things... but ALL for the good of those who love Him. How do I know this is true? Because I believe the Bible to be true with a capital T. I have seen with my own eyes how God has worked out difficult situations and trials for His good. Not only has this happened in my life, but it will happen in yours, as well. If it weren't for the operations I've had, if it weren't for my parents listening to God and not the doctors, I might not have been here today.

I tell you all this to say that God loves you and has great plans for you. My life has been pretty exciting, but it wasn't always joyful or happy. There were times when I was depressed, sad, angry, annoyed, and frustrated. We don't want to be in situations that make us feel like this. However, we all have to bear them sometimes. One of the most significant struggles in my life was having people call me names. I know bullying is a big issue in the world today, and for that I am sorry. I know how it is to be bullied. I know the hurt and the pain it brings to people. It's not always an easy thing to overcome.

There's an old saying you've probably heard that goes, "Sticks and stones may break my bones, but words will never hurt me." That's a lie from the pit of hell. If it was true, then why would so many people get upset when they are called a nasty name? It hurt when people would make fun of me or point and stare. I would rather people come up to me and talk to me just like they would anyone else. For the most part, people do not bully me anymore. However, there are still times when I walk by people and they whisper to each other. I always wonder, what did they just say? Are they talking about me? Why are they staring at me?

As I mentioned before, there were some times when I felt like I wanted to end my life. Could bullying be one of those reasons? Maybe. Could it also be that I was tired and frustrated with trying to figure out what it was that God had for me? Possibly. In the end, that still, small voice said to me, "Don't do it. I've got something better for you. Don't give up." Even now, when I feel like giving up on my traveling and speaking ministry, I feel the same still, small voice (that I know without a doubt is the Holy Spirit) saying to me, "Don't quit. Don't give up. I've got great things in store for your life."

I've heard people say that more and more churches are not bringing in guest speakers, evangelists, or missionaries. That would put the ministry I do at risk. However, God promises to open the doors that He wants open and close the doors that He wants closed. We can't be concerned about what will happen when we are walking in the will of God. We just have to trust in God and allow Him to accomplish what He has for us.

Proverbs 3:5-6 says, "Trust in the LORD with all your

heart and do not lean on your own understanding. In all your ways acknowledge Him, and He will make your paths straight" (NASB). When we wonder where we should go or what we should do with our lives, who to marry, what job to get, where to live, or what house to buy, we have to trust in God. When we do, "He will make [our] paths straight."

When I went into the operating room for any of my sixty-eight operations, I couldn't trust the doctors. I couldn't trust the nurses. I had to trust in God. It wasn't that I didn't think the doctors would be able to operate on me, but doctors aren't perfect. They make mistakes. They cannot be the objects of our faith – only God can be. While I was growing up, I had faith in God, but I didn't always trust Him securely. It's kind of like when you're holding someone's hand tightly. You have it firmly, and you know you're not going to let it go. I didn't trust God like that. I was holding onto Him too loosely. I think there are times when we are all like that, no matter how old or spiritually mature we are. None of us have our faith securely in God 24 hours a day, 365 days a year. However, we should always be striving to grow our faith and to become more like Him.

8

THE TEENAGE YEARS

I would say that, for most people, the teenager years are probably one of the most awkward times of life. I was no different, although I enjoyed my teenage years very much. There were certainly things I didn't enjoy, like having acne. Even so, I wanted to be treated the same as everyone else, and having acne was one way that I could be. I had to go to a dermatologist and put medicine on my face, just like many other teenagers. To this day, there are times that I have breakouts. They still bother me because I want to look "normal," and for the most part, adults don't have acne breakouts. But I try not to let it frustrate me too much.

Most students change schools when they finish elementary school and enter high school, but I didn't have to worry about that. The school I went to started in Pre-K and went all the way through twelfth grade. I never had to get acquainted with different kids because I always had the same classmates. The only thing that did change were the teachers, but even that wasn't too difficult to get used to. I especially loved my science and computer classes, but I missed the swimming classes I had when I was younger. People with disabilities want to be treated just like everyone else, and this school tried their best to do that. They even gave us a prom for both our junior and senior years in high school.

During my senior year, one of my most interesting experiences was going to Albany for our senior trip. Something happened that none of us was expecting – we got to meet the governor, George Pataki, and take pictures with him. Then, we all got sick and had to stay in our hotel rooms for most of the time. I'm not sure I'd say we had a great senior trip, but it did leave a lasting impact on many of us!

Sometimes, having a disability has its privileges because you get opportunities to meet interesting people or do interesting things. I loved that my school wanted to have a lot of the same activities that other schools offered, including Boy Scouts. It was just like regular Boy Scouts, but some of the activities had to be changed to accommodate those with disabilities. We would get badges and go camping. We even had pinewood derby races with wooden cars. One of my earliest memories from Boy Scouts was walking across the Brooklyn Bridge with the New York City Fire Department to make sure we stayed safe. We saw a fireboat on the water, and when we reached the other side of the bridge, there were TV cameras to interview those who had made the long trek. We got to meet Mayor Ed Koch, too. I can remember getting my picture taken with one of the firefighters – they even put a helmet on my head. That picture was displayed on a poster in several different firehouses.

Another time while I was with the Boy Scouts, I got picked to do a promo video for a charity. I came home one day from school, and my mom told me that I was going to meet a famous singer. I thought it would be someone I recognized or at least knew by name. Unfortunately, it wasn't. She told me it was going to be Tony Bennett. I was like, "Who is Tony Bennett?" I still enjoyed the experience, though.

Another interesting thing that happened while I was a teenager was when my parents and I decided to go to the city for dinner at Planet Hollywood. We went in and sat down at our table. After a few minutes, we noticed that there was someone in the restaurant who was being interviewed. We didn't know who he was, so we asked our waitress. She responded, "Oh, that's Matthew Perry." Turns out he was doing a promo video for a movie he was doing with Selma Hayek called "Fools Rush In." He was so nice! He came over and introduced himself. He even took a picture with me, which I still have to this day.

I remember playing floor hockey from the time I was in seventh grade until I finished high school. It was great, and I played with other students in the school who had disabilities. I don't recall ever winning the championship at the end of the year, but we still had a lot of fun.

One of the highlights of this experience was becoming the team captain.

One time when we were playing a game, I did something that most people usually avoid when they're playing a sport. I was trying to pass the plastic puck to my teammate. Unfortunately, I was so close to our team's net that it bounced off the goalie's wheelchair into the goal, scoring a point for the other team. Oh, well! Another of my best sports memories was when the NY Islanders came and played against us once every year. Playing floor hockey was definitely a wonderful experience!

I also enjoyed going to youth group when I was a teenager. I couldn't always be there, since the youth group met on the same night that I was involved with my hockey league. However, I always had a good time when I could go. On one of my birthdays, they threw a party and roasted me. Since I can't tie my shoes, one kid asked people to tie and untie his shoes so he could pretend he was me. He didn't really play me that well, but it was all in fun. They did it to show that they loved and cared for me.

Another fun thing I did while I was in the youth group was participate in holiday plays. I wasn't the best actor, so I never got the lead in any of the plays. One Christmas, however, they let me sing "Mary, Did You Know" with background vocals. How and why they let me do that, I have no idea. I cannot sing for my life! However, with God, all things are possible.

I participated in many of the youth group events –

conventions, winter retreats, and even a skiing trip one year. On the skiing trip, I was on one of the smaller slopes, and I can recall to this day that I went backward down the hill on my skis. Later on the trip, something must have scared me in my sleep, because I woke up, screamed "Mommy," and fell back to sleep. That's all I can remember.

As I got older and wanted to work with young people, I eventually became a youth leader. That was what really sparked my passion for working with the youth ministry. I remember talking to one of the other leaders one day about what I wanted to do, and he said, "I can see you onstage, giving your testimony." I was only seventeen or eighteen at the time, so I had no idea what God was calling me to do with my life. I should have told this youth leader that he was out of his mind, because I definitely did not see public speaking in my future. Looking back now, though, I know it's possible that God was using him to guide me.

Because I went to a school for people with special needs, seniors had to go through a process to decide what they would do after they graduated. My mom and I went to a meeting to discuss what I was going to do, and the idea of me going to college came up. My high school history teacher, Mr. K, was there. Someone asked him if he thought I would be able to go to college.

He said, "No. I don't think Dorsey would be able to make it in college."

You see, not everyone I went to school with had the

opportunity to go to college. Some of them went on to do vocational training. Some of them just went to live in group homes. I was one of the fortunate ones to even have the chance to go to college. Now, granted, I was not an A student. I needed some extra help in some subjects. However, like my parents taught me throughout life, I wanted to take the step and see what would happen if I did go. I told them I could make it through college because I believe that with God, all things are possible. Through that and my parents' support, I knew I would be able to succeed in higher education.

I graduated from the Henry Viscardi School in June of 1996. Then, I proved Mr. K wrong – I went to college.

9

MY COLLEGE LIFE

I can remember having a conversation with my mom before I went to college. We were talking about how long she thought it would take me to finish. My mom, being the big supporter that she was, said, "I don't care if it takes you ten years to finish college, as long as you finish." I don't know if that was just a wild guess or a fluke, but her prediction wasn't that far off. It took me four years at Queensborough and five years at the University of Valley Forge – nine years in total. That means I could've been a doctor, but once again, God had better plans in mind for my life.

I decided to major in liberal arts, but I had absolutely no idea what that meant. I was filled with questions. After two years of college, what job would I get? I had wanted to be a nurse when I was younger, but after realizing what I had to go through in the hospital, I ran away from that as quickly as I could.

Going to the same elementary, middle, and high

school for fourteen years was kind of like being in a bubble. I was there for a long time, and it was fairly easy. I knew everyone; I was acquainted with all the teachers, and I had friends. Going to college was an entirely different story. Transitioning from a familiar environment to a college filled with a couple thousand students made me feel like a fish transferring from a pond to the ocean. Regardless, I decided to enter Queensborough Community College in August of 1996. Walking into a community college where I didn't know anyone was very overwhelming for me. My biggest question was, "What did I get myself into?"

I remember the first day of community college. I had to take a placement exam. My dad was in the car, so I came walking out and told him I had to take a test already. For me, taking tests never came naturally. I always had a difficult time.

The first couple weeks weren't easy for me. I think that when I realized how many tests I'd have to take, papers I'd have to write, and assignments I'd have to study for, I became a little fearful. When I went home, I would often feel sick. I actually had a discussion with my parents about the possibility of quitting college and trying something else.

Even though I felt unwell and was tempted to drop out of college, I continued. I found Chi Alpha, a Christian club on campus, and decided I would attend their first meeting. After that first meeting with Chi Alpha, I was no longer sick. Sometimes, God brings people into our lives during difficult situations to help, encourage, and support us. This was one of those situations.

I remember talking to my mom about what it meant for me to be learning disabled. I never thought of myself like that, and I never would. I never wanted anything to hold me back from what God wanted to accomplish in my life, whether the limitation was my physical disability, my learning disability, or even an action I didn't think I could accomplish. Although I didn't want to identify myself by what held me back, I did become part of the disability group at school. That meant I would get extra help with some classes and individual tests.

Let me ask you a question. Are you allowing something in your life – whether it is big or small – to keep you from what God has for you?

There are times in our lives when we allow fear, doubt, or concern to hold us back from what God wants to do. Perhaps you are asking yourself, "How is God going to use me?" I've asked myself the same question: "God, what am I going to be able to do? What do you have in store for me?" Just know that God has given you talents, gifts, and dreams, just as He did for me. He wants to use you, like He is using me. Just as God answered some of my questions, He will answer yours, as well. One of the most difficult uncertainties in my life was how I was going to make it in college. But eventually, God gave me the answer to that question.

Although Queensborough was a two-year community college, it took me a little longer to finish than it would have taken others. I spent two additional years at the community college and really got to know some people. I'm still good friends with Kevin, one of the guys I met there. I even followed him to the University of Valley Forge. Kevin wanted to be a missionary to Africa, and I kidded around with him, saying I wouldn't be following him there. One time while we were at Queensborough, I remember Kevin telling me to be careful about looking at the girls while I was walking. The next day, I came in with a black and blue mark. When Kevin asked me what happened, I told him I had walked into a pole while I was saying goodbye to a girl the day before.

After graduating with an associate degree in liberal arts from Queensborough in May of 2000, I wanted to continue with my education at a Bible college. Maybe you're saying to yourself, "You just struggled with community college for four years. You probably had to repeat classes more than once. Why go on?" I went on because I believed that was what God had for me. I also knew that if He didn't want me to continue my education, He would eventually close that door. Although I didn't hear God's still, small voice telling me to continue, I decided to take the small step of faith to move forward and see what He would do with me at Bible college.

In the end, God never closed that door. He kept it open.

I entered the University of Valley Forge in August of 2000. When I got there, I found out that Kevin, my friend from Queensborough, was in the same dorm

I was. It may have been a coincidence, but I think he was just trying to punish me for following him there. I'm only kidding! It was certainly not a punishment; I thought it was great to already know someone at college. If Kevin were to tell you a story about what it was like to live near me, he'd probably bring up the time I woke him up early in the morning. I was talking on the phone next to a window that just happened to be right next to his room. But hey, I couldn't help it if he kept his window open while I was talking on the phone!

It was a great experience to meet others in the dorm and on campus. One fun thing was that the librarian had the same name as me – Dorsey Reynolds. So that was a running joke on campus.

Another guy I met was named Ricardo. He nicknamed me DROCK, and I never really knew why, but that was my nickname on campus. For the most part, everyone would call me that. My experience at Bible college was very different than the one I had at the community college, for sure. Although I had friends at Queensborough, UVF was a smaller community. I met a lot more people, especially since most of us lived on campus. We were also closer because all of us were Christians and had a lot in common. Because of this, I was able to foster lifelong friendships that I still have to this day. I have another friend, Dan Desrosiers, and to this day, he still teases me about how I sing. It isn't because I sing badly... well, actually, yes, it is. But it is also because I used to keep singing even after everyone else had stopped. When we sang the song "Doxology," he'd make fun of me because of my high pitch. He said he knew exactly where I was sitting in the room when we sang that song.

Another time, Dan and the other guys on my floor took every piece of furniture, including my bed, out of my room and put it in the lounge. It was all in fun, of course! Dan used to laugh at me because I wasn't able to operate the waffle maker correctly. I would have to get up early in the morning for class, so I tried to have breakfast around six o'clock. I remember knocking on the door of a guy named Adam Barnes, and he would throw his shoes at me. Regardless of the jokes and pranks that the guys at school played on me, I can honestly say that they were always there for me, especially when my mom passed away.

One of the hardest things in my life that I had to deal with happened in August of 2002. I got a call from my dad. He said that Mom was in the hospital. She had suffered a stroke. I knew that when it comes to health problems – especially severe ones – we can fight them with God's help until He calls us home. When we have a relationship with Christ, passing away is not a total loss. It's a win-win situation, because when that person passes away, they are on the other side of eternity. Eventually, we will see them again.

I have always been close to my mom. She always stayed with me in the hospital or walked me to the door of the operating room. We'd talk almost every day when

I was in high school. I would sometimes even go to the payphone and call her just to say hello. To say that I was a "mama's boy" is probably an understatement. My mom and I talked often even while I was in Bible college. So, when I tried to call her one day and couldn't get her on the phone, I knew something wasn't right.

On December 7, 2002, I remember getting a phone call from my sister. She told me that Mom had passed away due to complications from the stroke. At that time, I was reading a book by Kathy Troccoli called *Am I Not Still God?* I remember throwing the book across the room. More than likely, I was thinking, "How are you still God when you've taken my mom away from me?"

My mom was my biggest supporter and encourager. Along with my dad, she was always there for me. Three days after she passed away, we had her funeral. A lot of college students would have taken the rest of the semester off if they had just lost their mom. I could've done that to grieve my mom's passing. It would have been understandable. Sometimes things happen in our lives that we can't grasp, and we need that time to process it.

However, instead of doing that, I decided to go back and finish the semester. I even returned for the next one. I could've gotten angry at God for taking my mom when she was still so young, but I didn't. I wanted to persevere and keep doing what God wanted me to do. I also knew that if I quit college, I would have disappointed my mom. So, I continued.

Fortunately, I had a professor, Darren Hileman,

whose mom had also passed away at a young age. He told me that when I prayed, I should ask Jesus to say "hello" to my mom for me and tell her I'm thinking of her. That helped to comfort me during my time of loss.

I was studying to be a youth pastor, and just like in high school and community college, I struggled with some of my classes. I even had to retake parts of the Greek and Hebrew classes three different times. I didn't always do that well in school. I even met with some of my advisors about whether or not I should get my associate degree, just in case I wasn't able to graduate with a bachelor's.

Throughout my five years at Bible college, I had to do two internships. One was relatively small, and I was able to serve in a church at home where I had gotten to know the pastor a few years before. He was the youth pastor, and I helped him out during the summer. His name was Dominick Cotignola, but everyone called him PD. During one service, I got the opportunity to give a sermon to the youth group. I had invited a friend of mine to come and hear me that night. As we were driving away afterward, we talked about how it went. She asked me if I thought this was what I wanted to do. I said it was. Then, she told me that she didn't think my sermon had gone all that well. That felt like a kick in the gut to me. I was taken aback, but I refused to let it stop me. I had to keep going and see exactly what God had in store for my life.

You might wonder what kept me going. After all, many people had said things like that to me. My high school teacher, Mr. K, said I wouldn't make it in college. Many of my classmates made fun of me. This friend told me my sermon didn't go well. What was it that stopped me from quitting? The answer I always have is that it was God. My parents certainly encouraged me, but they always pointed me back to God. For the most part, whatever my friends said to me also pointed back to God. It's not bad to ask for advice from people, but the most important thing to do when you're not sure where to go is to get down on your knees and ask God to show you what *He* would have you do. That's what I did.

I knew I needed to figure out for myself if I was doing God's will. That's why I love Jeremiah 29:11 so much: "'For I know the plans that I have for you,' declares the LORD, 'plans for welfare and not for calamity to give you a future and a hope'" (NASB). God does have plans for us. He does have hope for us. He does have a future for us. As Jeremiah 29:10 says, it may take up to seventy years for Him to answer, but He will. Often, when we pray, we think we should get the answer immediately and exactly the way we want. That's not always the case. God works in His timing and in His way. Our prayers aren't always answered the way we think they should be.

I could've looked back and thought about when Mr. K told me I'd never make it in college. Most people probably didn't think I would be able to. Doctors, teachers, and maybe even some professors thought I wouldn't get through higher education. In fact, the doubt even crossed my mind a time or two. But whenever I contemplated quitting, I reminded myself that I needed to press forward. Thankfully, I didn't give up – not even when my mom passed away.

Twenty-eight years after birth, nine years after graduating from high school, and three years after I lost my mom, I crossed the stage at the University of Valley Forge to receive my Bachelor of Arts degree in Youth Ministry. That was May 5, 2005.

For those of you who are struggling with college, you can do it. For those of you who are thinking of quitting, don't. Press on and see what God can do in your life. Some of you may have been told, like me, that you wouldn't make it. That may be ingrained in your mind. But you should at least try. Take that first step onto campus. Take the next. Then, see where God will lead you. That's what I had to do, especially when it came time to interview for jobs after college.

Both before and after graduation, I went to several interviews to become a youth pastor. After each interview, the door was closed. I started to wonder if this was happening because I had a disability and a speech impediment. Why weren't my interviewers giving me a call back? Why weren't they continuing the interview process? I remember that one pastor I interviewed with told me that my disability wouldn't be a factor in their decision. Even still, I did not get a call back or any information about why they would not hire me.

Looking back, I can see now that God was working in each stage of the job search process. It was frustrating and often disappointing not to get hired as a youth pastor, but I understand now why it happened – because God had a calling for my life. I may not have seen it back when I was in college, and I may not have realized that God would have me travel as an evangelist and give my testimony, but God knew.

I think sometimes we put God in a box. We try to limit what He can and cannot do. When a door closes, we think that's the end of God's plan in that situation, and it may be. This thing may not have been God's will to begin with. At the time, we get frustrated and disappointed, but that's only because we forget that God sees the bigger picture. I thought I knew what God had in store for me after graduation, but I didn't. When I didn't get a job, I decided to go home. I didn't know where else I was supposed to be.

When I got home, I went back to my church, but just didn't feel the support or encouragement I was looking for. So, what did I do? I decided to go to Bellerose Assembly of God. That was one of the churches where I had an internship during my years at the University of Valley Forge. I also knew the youth pastor from both community college and Bible college – my friend, Kevin Bateman.

This was the same guy I said I wouldn't follow to Africa. Instead, I just followed him to Bellerose Queens.

10

LIVING WITH APERT SYNDROME

Not only did I follow my friend Kevin to Bellerose, but I also got to meet up with a friend of mine named Efrain Figueroa. He and I had met at Bethlehem Assembly of God, where I previously attended, and I served as a leader under him. To be honest, I'm not sure how he and I are friends, since he is an Oakland Raiders fan and I am a Broncos fan, but we manage. Efrain became a pastor at Bellerose, so when I got there, it was like a big family reunion. At this point, I still wanted to work with youth; I didn't know that God had an entirely different plan for my life.

I remember one time when Efrain took me out to discuss what God wanted to do with me in more detail. Efrain (or Pastor E., as I called him) drove me to a Dunkin Donuts, and he told me that God was going to do great and amazing things in my life. That weekend, we went on a retreat with the young adults. Pastor E. had to go home early because his wife went into labor.

When I got home, Pastor E. called and said, "You'll never guess what happened!" Of course, I was intrigued. He said that he had gotten a knock on his front door from the NYPD anti-terrorist squad, who questioned him about the person he was talking to that day at Dunkin Donuts.

Now, I've been called a lot of things, but a terrorist... well, that was a first.

I tell you this story to say that Pastor E., like so many of my close friends, never sees me as someone with a disability. He just sees me. When the anti-terrorist squad questioned him, he didn't even realize who they were talking about at first. Thankfully, he was eventually able to assure them, and that was the end of that.

The pastors at Bellerose always supported my desire to get into the ministry. Sometimes, they were even more optimistic than I was. It seemed to me like doors were always closing, and that was frustrating and disappointing at times. It's easy to forget the verse in Matthew 7:7 (AMP) that says, "Ask and keep on asking and it will be given to you. Seek and keep on seeking and you will find; knock and keep on knocking and the door will be opened to you." I love this verse because it talks about asking, seeking, and knocking on the door in prayer to God. We need to ask Him for what we want, according to His will.

The continuous knocking refers to persevering. If you know me at all, then you know I'm persistent. I don't give up on anything very easily. When doors for ministry kept on closing, I could easily have said, "Okay, God. I give up. I don't know what I was doing at UVF for the last five years, but now I give up." But I didn't, because I believed in Matthew 7:7. I believed that God would eventually open up the right door at the right time. There was a professor at UVF named Dr. David Dippold, and I heard him speak about this verse once. He said, "You can't just ask, seek, and knock one time. It has to be a continuous asking, seeking, and knocking in prayer. That's what you have to do to find out what God has for your life."

I am so grateful for the support group of pastors at Bellerose and their continual encouragement of me in this ministry. I started by helping out with the youth group until it was time for me to move on to the next thing God wanted me to do. That's the way it happens sometimes. We think we're ready and we think it's the right time for God to use us in some big way, but we forget that God is always an on-time God. Where He has us right now is where He wants us, and He will lead us to the next stage when the time is right.

Throughout my life, I have been able to meet a lot of people with Apert, even though it is a rare condition. I met several children when I stayed at the hospital. For several years, I even went to school with a young woman who had Apert. I've met several people through Facebook, too.

At one point, I met a young man named Adam Hogan, and we grew to be close friends. I went to Maryland to visit him. We went out to dinner, and at the restaurant, the waiter asked us if we were twins. That's how close of a resemblance we have to each other. When people have disabilities, they usually don't look alike. That's not the case with Apert. Another time when Adam and I went out, I hit on the waitress. Regardless of everything that has happened in my life, nothing will stop me from talking to ladies and trying to find the right one.

One of my other friends with Apert is Tom Gardner. He lives in Plymouth, England. We met on Facebook, and at one point, he came to see me in New York while visiting his family in the States. We had a great time visiting the city and getting to know each other. We even went to the Bubba Gump restaurant for lunch. I hope to one day go over to visit him in England and possibly even speak at his church. Then I would be an international evangelist.

Since we have the same disabilities, my friends and I have been through many similar experiences. It's nice to be able to share these things with people who understand. I love all of my friends, but most of them find it hard to understand everything I've gone through. They really can't unless they have a disability, too. It's nice to be able to talk to someone who knows what it's like to be made fun of or to not be able to do something. We talk about how it will be to live alone at some point in our lives, too. That's one of my biggest dreams. I want to be able to live on my own. I know others with various disabilities also feel the same way. We want to have the freedoms that everyone else has.

Once, during my travels, I met a parent whose young child had Apert. Unfortunately, this child's case was much more severe than mine. He had to have a breathing tube. He will probably have difficulty hearing for most of his life. Our stories were similar in that this child's doctors told his mother the same thing my doctors told my parents. They said he would not survive, but he did. In the time since I met this little boy, I've lost contact with his mom, but I do know that God had His hand on the child's life. Living with a disability is not easy. It's very difficult to deal with your emotions, your physical limitations, or your spiritual life. However, God has helped me to overcome these problems. I have learned (and am still learning) that we will have trials and difficulties in this world. However, Jesus says in John 16:33 that we are to take heart, because He has overcome the world. When we're living for Him, we will have trouble, but we will also have peace.

John 16:33 (AMP): "'I have told you these things, so that in Me you may have [perfect] peace. In the world you will have tribulation and distress and suffering, but be courageous [be confident, be undaunted, be filled with joy]; I have overcome the world.' [My conquest is accomplished, My victory abiding.]"

With all that I have gone through and will go through in my life, it is easy to become afraid or anxious. That's because we don't always know what is ahead. I certainly don't. I am living with a birth defect that the doctors don't always understand or fully comprehend. I'm sure that when I was born, my parents were fearful. They didn't know what to expect. There are times in my life when I don't know what is going to happen. My dad was dealing with a heart issue for a while. Although he and my mom took care of me for most of my younger life, it became my responsibility to take care of him with the help of my sister. It was difficult to know what would happen with my dad. Would he come out of this? If so, how? However, as I said before, I had to trust in God, have faith in Him, and know that God would work it all out in the end.

In the end, God did work it all out. Even though I was worried and fearful, God brought my dad through. He had AFIB, but after a procedure, he came out with a normal rhythm. Some people would say this procedure fixed my dad's problem. I believe by faith that God healed my father while he was undergoing the procedure.

Other times, I get worried about the things I find on my body. For example, once I found a mark on my face. I thought it looked abnormal, so I went to the doctor. He examined me and found that it was nothing. I go through that kind of thing a lot, and it's easy to allow worry to take over.

The phrases "do not fear" or "fear not" are found many times in the Bible. One example is Philippians 4:6 (NASB): "Be anxious for nothing, but in everything by prayer and supplication with thanksgiving let your requests be made known to God." The word that is used there is not "fear," but it does command us not to be anxious. When trouble or hard times come, we are not to be afraid. When a loved one is in the hospital, like my father was, the Bible says "do not be anxious." When you are living with a disability and times get tough, do not fear – do not be anxious. At times like these, we are to pray. We are to seek the face of God, and when we do, a peace from God will come upon us so that we will not fear, but have peace. When that peace comes, it will help to guard our hearts and minds in Christ Jesus.

I have prayed about many things in my life, especially when I have been anxious. When I pray, God's peace comes upon me, and that helps me to realize He has it all under control; it's all in His hands. Next time you feel fearful about something in your life, do not worry; pray. Ask God to bring you the peace which surpasses all understanding to guard your heart and mind from all anxiety.

Even though living with a disability is hard sometimes, I have found ways to live with it. It's hard not to get angry or frustrated, and I've had to work on not being bitter toward God. There are times when I worry about things that happen to me physically. The fact is that I don't want to die young. I've known so many people with disabilities, and they often die at a young age. I don't want that to happen to me. I want to live to a normal age. For the most part, that is a possibility for people with Apert. However, when you've seen people die young, it sticks with you. At the same time, I realize there is a time and a place for everything, and

I know that God has it all set up. He knows when I am going to die. No matter when or how that happens, everything that happens is in God's time and plan, and that is good.

11

Finding My Calling

I had come home from Bible college in the summer of 2005 after I was unable to find a youth ministry position. Ever since I started at the University of Valley Forge, I had thought that God wanted me to be a youth pastor, and at this point, I still thought so. Why things hadn't worked out yet, I had no idea. At one point, my former youth pastor, Efrain Figueroa, told me he wanted me to go out to the Dream Center in California to see if I could do ministry out there. However, I didn't want to go at that time because I was living with my dad, and he was getting older. I wanted to stay home so I could be close to him.

While I was home, I went back to my old school and volunteered there with my elementary school teacher, who taught second, third, and fourth grade. Eventually, I found out the school had an opening for someone to work on the smart boards and handle any complications that arose with the computers. I did that for about nine months until the funding ran out for the project. After that, I decided to leave the school. It was around the holidays, so I applied for jobs at retail stores. Finally, one of the stores hired me, and I started working there in December of 2006.

In May of 2006, I got my minister's license from the New York District of the Assemblies of God. As you can see, I've never let anything stop me from doing whatever God wanted me to do. I am grateful for this, and I am hopeful as I look forward to the next experiences God has for me.

During the summer of 2006, while I was still home looking for a ministry opportunity, my pastor, Dominick Cotignola, wanted to do an outreach event called Summerfest for the community. He called on people within the church to help, and we needed a lot of volunteers for skits, music, videos, and all kinds of activities. At one point, he asked people to volunteer to give their testimony. I had my minister's license, but I didn't want to seem pushy. As an introvert, I was often hesitant to put myself out there. Nevertheless, I went up and talked to him about it.

God works everything out in His timing. If you think that God is not on time or that you missed His plan and purpose for your life, that's not true. Pastor Dom decided that he would allow me to give my testimony via video at the outreach, which I did.

Even though I was doing the video testimony for the outreach, I still wondered what God had for me and how

He was going to use me long-term for the ministry. One day, I was in my room praying, and I felt the Holy Spirit say to me, "Send this out and see what I will do with it." I realized that He meant for me to send out the video I had made for the outreach event to different pastors and organizations to see if they would allow me to come and share my testimony at their service. Sometimes, God calls us to walk by faith and not by sight (2 Corinthians 5:7). I had no idea what I was doing. I had no clue that God was going to call me to travel around, giving my testimony.

I met with my pastor and the Superintendent of the New York District, Duane Durst. They both thought that sharing my story was a great idea, and they gave me their blessing. I started working and making phone calls in February of 2007. At the same time, I was still employed at the retail store. I wanted to work in the toy department. I figured that would be the most chaotic and fun place to work, especially during Christmastime. However, they ended up putting me in the furnishing department. It wasn't nearly as fun as the toy department would have been, but it wasn't too bad.

The retail store sent me a letter at the end of the Christmas season saying they wanted to keep me on as a part-time employee once the holidays were over. I decided to stay, although it wasn't exactly what I wanted to do. It wasn't the most enjoyable job, but it was okay. I dealt with it. Eventually, I was moved up to a cashier position. Why the employers would ever decide to move a young adult with a disability and only nine fingers (and shortened ones at that) to a cashier position is beyond me.

Nevertheless, having a disability caused me to be open about my life, which provided opportunities to share what God had done for me with the people I met. There were very few people I worked with who didn't know I was a Christian. I wasn't a Bible thumper, and I didn't sit down in the break room and try to get them all saved, but they knew who and what I was. There were times when I had to travel on the weekends, and God gave me favor with management when I asked them only to schedule me for weekdays. There I was, traveling as an evangelist, speaking around the area where I lived, and working in a retail store.

On October 31, 2008, I was working my cashier shift like I normally did, and one of the employees who didn't know me looked over and said, "Hey, why don't you take off your mask?" Now, mind you, no one else was wearing a mask, and at first, I thought he was kidding. If he had been a friend of mine, maybe I would have taken it as a joke. But I didn't. I was taken aback by his question, but tried to ignore it. However, he said it again a second time. I decided to step away from the situation, but I got angry when I went back into the break room. I said something that I more than likely shouldn't have said.

Yes, me. The minister. The one who listens to Christian music. I said something I probably shouldn't have said because I'm a human being and I make mistakes, just like everyone else. Thankfully, the Bible tells us in 1 John 1:9 that "If we confess our sins, He is faithful and righteous to forgive us our sins and to cleanse us from all unrighteousness."

As an adult, I was used to people saying things like my fellow employee had said. Usually, it didn't bother me, but this particular time, it did. It got to me so much that I decided to go into the Human Resources office and hand in my notice. Two weeks later, I walked out of the retail store, never to look back again. Was it a wise move? I don't know. Either way, I know God supplied every need I had. My dad was there for me, of course, but God is the one who ultimately provided.

Even though I was no longer working my retail job, I still had the ministry. I was still traveling around, speaking at different churches. This time, they were churches outside of New York in states like Connecticut, New Jersey, and Pennsylvania. Depending on how far the trip was, my dad would sometimes come with me. For the first couple of years, I didn't have a whole lot of speaking dates, but as time went on, God continued to open up more and more opportunities.

During that same year, 2008, there was a time I had some issues with my stomach. The symptoms didn't go away, so I finally found a doctor who ordered me to have an endoscopy. Some tests aren't very easy to go through, and this one was no exception. Afterward, I found out that I had a constriction that wasn't allowing food to go down directly into my stomach. The doctor decided he would give me medicine to see what would happen. I still have the issue, and I also have a Barrett's esophagus. I believe that God will provide complete healing. Still, I know it is wise to go to the doctor. At one point, the doctor was surprised because I wasn't having any symptoms. He said, "I will knock on wood." I told him, "No, I believe God will heal me, just as He will eventually stop the seizures I've always had." I have always trusted God for my healing, even when I was growing up. I used to pray for God to completely heal my body, even my face and hands. Although He hasn't completely healed me, He has taken away some of my symptoms many times. Regardless of whether it is here on earth or in heaven, I am confident that He will ultimately heal me. I have great faith!

In 2009, I was ordained as a pastor, which is the highest level of licensing you can receive. I went to the ordination with Pastor Dom and Kevin. It's always a great thing to have friends, especially those like Dom and Kevin, who have loved, cared for, and supported me throughout the years. They have always been a great encouragement to me when things are going well. Then, when things are tough and I am frustrated, they are there to help and support me in the ministry. For these things, I am grateful.

As my ministry continued, one of my greatest experiences was going to Wisconsin to speak at the Special Touch Ministry Camp in March of 2009. Special Touch is a camp for people with disabilities. I met the director of the camp, Charlie Chivers, and some of the campers, too. Then, I had the opportunity to speak to them and learn about what they've been through and what God was doing in their lives. The craziest thing about this trip was that I flew out of New York, and most of the time, New York is warm by that time of year. I didn't even think that Wisconsin might be much colder, but it was! I actually had to borrow someone's coat for a few days while I was there.

Another great trip I took was to Sacramento, California, to go and speak at Capital Christian Center. I also had plenty of time to go sightseeing, since I was there for four days. Speaking at the church and exploring the area were not the highlights of this trip for me, though.

The Friday I was there, I was able to be part of a prom that the church put on for people with disabilities. The theme for that night was American Idol, and people with all types of disabilities came. They received the red-carpet treatment, too! They got to ride in limousines and exotic cars. There was a DJ and dance floor, too. I couldn't resist; I just had to dance! It was so great to see a church put on a prom for people who probably would never have been able to experience something like that. I was fortunate that I went to a school for people with disabilities that held proms. I'm not quite sure that I would have gone to the prom if I had attended a regular school.

God has opened up many doors for me through my speaking ministry. He has allowed me to be interviewed on TBN, to give my testimony, to write my story for a Christian magazine, and to travel this country – and only He knows what else He has in store for my future. You may be wondering what God has for you. You may not see it, and you may not know what it is at the moment, but God has something in store for your life. God says in His Word that no one knows exactly what the future will hold. You may be going through a lot in your life right now, and you might not be able to see God in the battles you are facing. Maybe you feel like giving up, as I did so many times. Let me encourage you – don't give up on the hope that God has for you. Know this today, that since the day you were born, God had your life and your future all planned out.

Epilogue

My pastor always says, "The best is yet to come." No, he's not talking about the song by Frank Sinatra. He's saying that although we've already had good things in our lives, even better things are coming because God is the one who has them planned for us. Throughout my life, I never thought that there would be great things coming for me. With the operations, the bullying, and the people telling me I wouldn't make anything of myself, I often wondered what would happen in my life. However, as you can see, with God's help and grace, I have been able to dispel the lies of the enemy. Instead of believing what people had told me, I started to believe what God told me – and that was that He had good things in store for my life.

This is not only true for me, but for you, as well. Maybe you, too, look at your life and say, "I didn't always have good things; how do I know that greater things are coming?" My answer to that is... I don't know. But I'm believing it by faith for both you and me. We don't know what's going to happen tomorrow. That is why God says we cannot worry about tomorrow, for today has enough trouble of its own. Unfortunately, regardless of whether or not we are Christians, we will all face trials and tribulations in our lives. However, I know one thing – God will be there for me, and He will protect, guide, and help me through the challenges I will experience. If you know Him, He will do the same for you.

Although I have had health issues since childhood and have had doctors tell me that I would die at a certain age, I hope to live a lot longer than just forty-three. Maybe I'll even surpass the age of normalcy for people with my disability. Could it be that the greater thing that is coming in my life is that I will do a lot more traveling and one day become an international evangelist? I would like to go and see my friend Tom in England. I'm not sure what exactly is going to happen, but I'm not going to say, "Woe is me." I'm going to continue to use my saying, "'Can't' is not in my vocabulary," and believe that there are greater things that will come in my life.

If you get anything from this book, I hope you hear me saying that God is an amazing God. To this day, He still does great and wonderful things in our lives. I also hope that after reading this book, you say, "If Dorsey can have faith in God and not give up on his life after what he's been through, so can I." Remember that God has an amazing plan and purpose for your life, as He does for me. Not only that, but better things are coming in your future. I can't tell you what they are, but I believe by faith that they are coming. How do I know? Because they came for me. Maybe God did not give me exactly what I was hoping for, but He gave me what He knew was best in His perfect timing. The questions that we ask and the prayers that we pray are important, but we must also realize that in the end, God will work out every circumstance for our good.

We have all thought about what is going to happen in the future. We all have dreams and visions for what we want to do in our lives. However, it's not really up to us, because God is the only one who knows what the future holds.

Maybe you're going through a dark time right now. I know what that's like. I have been there, and I will be there again at some point. That's because life is like a roller coaster ride; it has its ups and downs. But realize this – there are greater things in store for you, and the best is yet to come.

There's a saying that goes, "If being a Christian was easy, everyone would do it." Looking back over my life, it may have been hard, but I wouldn't change a thing about it. You can't look back and think, "Man, I wish I had done this differently or made a different choice in that situation." If you do, you won't ever look to the future. I have made mistakes and wrong decisions in my life, but I have learned from them and moved on. I'm thankful to God for where I have been, for where I am, and for the excitement of where I will be going in the future.

And remember – this is true for you, too. God has greater things in store for your life, greater things that are yet to come.

Made in the USA
Middletown, DE
15 February 2022